D1119284

moroccan café

Valérie Lhomme wishes to thank Marine Labrune for her priceless and enthusiastic assistance as well as the following shops for their willing cooperation: In the town of Mogador, Mèdina; Richbond, Rive Sud (located in Paris).

The editor wishes to thank Édouard Collet, Christine Martin and Mélanie Joly for their valuable aid and Marine Barbier for her careful reading.

casual moroccan cooking at home

moroccan café

Elisa Vergne

Photographs by Pierre Desgrieux
Design by Valérie Lhomme

[When the flavors blend …]

To everyone's delight, national borders are slowly disappearing in matters of cuisine. As the new century gets underway, we're witnessing a gradual acceptance of new culinary habits. We don't talk about "exotic cuisine" anymore because exotic means faraway, strange, and not necessarily authentic. We no longer consider Chinese, Indian or Mexican food to be unusual fare. The sources of inspiration for our cooking no longer matter as long as the results are delicious. It used to be that trying our hand at foreign cuisine was considered audacious, daring, but today it's part of our everyday lives. Ingredients that, in the past, had to be tracked with the skill of a detective or brought back by travelling friends, are now available locally from the neighborhood supermarket or even our corner grocer. We are no longer intimidated by peculiar spices, mysterious jars, or colorful fruits—but instead—we are learning how to use them. The world is coming to us and its flavors are being awakened in our kitchens. At the same time, we're discovering different ways of eating as well as dietary principles and eating habits from other countries. Our kitchens have become the melting pot for a natural blending of tastes; what was once quite curious is now so familiar that we forget its origins are foreign.

Of all the cuisines of North Africa, Moroccan cuisine is the one most influenced by aristocratic tradition. Through the centuries it has become steeped in heritage and nobility, consisting of dishes that are made to linger over. Moroccan cuisine is rooted in Medieval Spanish history; beginning with the Andalusian Muslims who achieved a highly sophisticated lifestyle further enriched by Islamic and Jewish influences. Even today, Muslims become nostalgic at the very mention of al Andalus. The recipes of ancient Andalusia have been the inspiration for Morocco's complex, flavorful, intoxicating dishes, all of which are prepared with great love and devotion. Inside the home, cooking is the province of women— flaky pastillas, slowly simmered tagines, light and sweet pastries. Outside the home, Moroccan cuisine is what can be found in the markets and fairs, just as it has evolved and is eaten in the streets. In the early morning hours, lambs are slowly roasted in sealed clay ovens. Every evening during Ramadan, the day's fast is broken with harira soup served from market stalls. And brochettes are available everywhere for casual nibbling. The great tradition of Moroccan cuisine lives on in the ancient, historic cities of Fès, Marrakesh and Meknès. You too can prepare these seductive dishes that will entrance all who partake of them. Your Moroccan dinners will be an experience your guests will not soon forget.

contents

first courses & soups   8

tagines   30

couscous & brochettes   50

pastillas & briouats   72

desserts   94

glossary   116

index   118

first courses & soups

first courses & soups

ritual and
pleasure

Moroccan soups are often hearty dishes made for serving during the evenings of Ramadan as a means of restoring body and soul. Salads, on the other hand, are bright oases that provide refreshment to the spice-laden meals. Although the combinations of ingredients are sometimes surprising, the result is always delicious as well as easy to make. These salads should be prepared well in advance and marinated to achieve the optimal fusion of flavors.

Serves 4–6
Prep time: 15 minutes
Marinating time: 2 hours

½ pound black olives
2 lemons
1 clove garlic (optional)
1 teaspoon paprika or
  mild chili powder
1 pinch hot chili powder
3 pinches ground cumin
1 tablespoon olive oil

[olive salad]

Rinse olives and dry thoroughly in paper towels.

Peel and coarsely chop lemons, carefully removing all pith and seeds. If applicable, peel garlic clove and squeeze through a garlic press. Mix all ingredients in a large bowl and marinate for 2 hours in a cool place.

Instead of lemons, you can use 1 or 2 oranges depending on their size.

[potatoes with spices and cilantro]

Serves 4–5
Prep time: 20 minutes
Cooking time: 1 hour

2 pounds boiling potatoes
2 tomatoes
3 onions
2 cloves garlic
3 sprigs fresh parsley
3 sprigs fresh cilantro
3 tablespoons olive oil
1 bay leaf
1 pinch ground ginger
1 pinch ground cumin
2 pinches paprika
Salt and pepper
1 small fresh chile pepper

Peel potatoes, wash and cut into round slices. Plunge tomatoes into boiling water for 10 seconds, then into cold water and peel. Remove seeds and chop flesh with a knife. Peel onions and cut into thin cross sections. Peel garlic cloves and squeeze through a garlic press. Wash parsley and cilantro, pat dry and chop leaves.

Heat oil in a sauté pan or saucepan with a thick base. When very hot, add onions and sauté for 5 minutes. Add round potato slices, chopped tomato flesh, garlic and the bay leaf and sprinkle with ginger, cumin, paprika and chopped herbs. Season with salt and pepper.

Add 1¼ cups water to contents of sauté pan and stir thoroughly. Cover and simmer for 45 minutes over low heat.

Remove chile pepper stem and seeds wearing gloves or under cold running water, then cut into thin cross sections. Add chile pepper to sauté pan and simmer for another 15 minutes.

[north african vegetable soup]

Peel and chop onions. Clean leeks, split in half, cut into round slices and wash. Peel potatoes, carrots and turnips and dice. Plunge tomatoes into boiling water for 10 seconds, then immediately into cold water, peel and chop flesh with a knife. Cut celery stalks into thin cross sections.

In a stockpot, melt butter. When it becomes foamy, sauté onions and leeks without browning them. Add potatoes and stock and bring to a boil.

Now add carrots, turnips, tomatoes and celery to stockpot. Use the salt sparingly, since stock is already salted, and season generously with pepper. Add turmeric, stir and cover. Bring to a boil again and then cook for another 20 minutes.

Sprinkle vermicelli in the soup and boil for another 5 minutes.

Wash parsley and cilantro, pat dry carefully and chop the leaves. Pour soup into a tureen, sprinkle with chopped parsley and cilantro, and serve immediately.

Serves 6
Prep time: 25 minutes
Cooking time: 40 minutes

2 large onions
4 leeks (white part only)
2 potatoes
4 carrots
2 turnips
4 tomatoes
2 stalks celery
4 tablespoons butter
2 quarts beef stock
Salt and black pepper
1 teaspoon turmeric
4 ounces vermicelli
4 sprigs fresh parsley
4 sprigs fresh cilantro

[stuffed artichokes]

Serves 6
Prep time: 45 minutes
Cooking time: 55 minutes

6 large artichokes
3 tablespoons lemon juice
8 ounces boneless shoulder
  of lamb
1 hard-cooked egg
3 sprigs fresh parsley
5 cloves garlic
1 egg
Salt and pepper
3 pinches turmeric
2 tablespoons olive oil

Cut off top third of artichoke leaves. Remove outer crown of leaves, then cut off base. Remove center. As you finish each one, place it in a bowl of water to which you have added 1 tablespoon of the lemon juice.

Chop meat. Peel hard-cooked egg and chop. Chop parsley. Peel and chop 2 of the garlic cloves over a bowl and add meat, hard-cooked egg, turmeric, parsley and raw egg. Season with salt and pepper and knead all the ingredients together.

Peel remaining garlic cloves and in a sauté pan, sauté them in oil. When they turn light gold, add 1¼ cups water, the remaining lemon juice, salt and pepper, and slowly bring to a boil.

Drain artichokes and stuff with filling. Place in the sauté pan, cover and simmer for 50 minutes over low heat. Test doneness by piercing them with the tip of a knife.

Arrange artichokes on a serving dish. Reduce sauce if you have too much and pour it over the artichokes. Serve warm.

[lettuce and orange salad]

Serves 4
Prep time: 15 minutes

2 heads romaine lettuce
2 oranges
1 tablespoon lemon juice
1 tablespoon orange
  blossom water
Salt
1 tablespoon sugar
Pepper
2 tablespoons olive oil

Clean lettuce and keep only the tender leaves. Wash these leaves, dry and cut into strips. Squeeze juice from 1 orange. Peel the other orange down to the flesh, carefully removing all pith, cut into round slices, remove seeds and then dice slices.

Combine orange juice, lemon juice and orange blossom water in a small bowl. Add 1 pinch salt, sugar and pepper. Mix thoroughly with a fork to dissolve the sugar, add olive oil and briskly emulsify dressing.

Place strips of romaine in a large salad bowl, add diced orange, pour on contents of dressing and toss. Serve chilled.

[hummus]

Place chickpeas in a bowl of cold water to which you have added kosher salt and soak for 12 hours. The next day, pour contents of bowl into a saucepan and boil for 5 minutes. Drain chickpeas and rub them between the palms of your hands to remove skins.

Peel and chop onion and garlic. In a saucepan, combine chickpeas, several pinches chili powder and cilantro. Cover with a generous amount of cold water and bring to a boil. Simmer for at least 2 hours, adding salt and pepper after 1 hour.

Remove cilantro, drain chickpeas and purée. Serve cold, garnished with cilantro.

Serves 6
Prep time: 15 minutes
Soaking time: 12 hours
Cooking time: 2 hours

1 pound chickpeas
 (garbanzo beans)
½ teaspoon kosher salt
1 large onion
1 clove garlic
Chili powder
2 sprigs fresh cilantro
Salt and pepper
Cilantro for garnish

[carrot salad]

Serves 4
Prep time: 10 minutes
Cooking time: 20 minutes

1¼ pounds carrots
3 cloves garlic
3 tablespoons vinegar
Ground cumin
  (about ½ teaspoon)
Chili powder
Salt and pepper
2 tablespoons olive oil
2 sprigs fresh parsley
2 sprigs fresh cilantro

Peel carrots, wash and cut into quarters lengthwise. Crush garlic cloves.

In a saucepan, bring some water to a boil, add carrots and garlic and boil for about 20 minutes.

Carefully drain carrots and place in a shallow bowl, and sprinkle with vinegar.

Season to taste with ground cumin, chili powder, salt, pepper and olive oil.

Wash parsley and cilantro, pat dry, chop and sprinkle over carrots. Toss just before serving. May be sprinkled with fennel seeds and garnished with cilantro or parsley, if desired.

[spicy sweet potatoes]

Serves 4
Prep time: 10 minutes
Cooking time: 30 minutes

1¼ pounds sweet potatoes
3 tablespoons oil
1 jar saffron
½ teaspoon ground
  cinnamon
1 tablespoon sugar
4 teaspoons butter
Salt and pepper

Peel sweet potatoes, and wash under running water, pat dry and cut into pieces. In a saucepan with a thick base, combine oil, saffron, cinnamon, sugar, butter and 2 pinches salt. Season generously with pepper. When spiced oil is very hot, add sweet potato pieces and ½ cup water. Cover and simmer for 30 minutes over medium heat.

If too much water remains at the end of the cooking time, uncover and reduce a little longer. Serve hot or cold.

[parsley salad]

Serves 3–4
Prep time: 10 minutes

1 large bunch very fresh
  Italian parsley
1 medium-sized white onion
2 large lemons
Salt

Wash parsley and dry thoroughly in paper towels. Finely chop leaves. Peel onion, quarter and thinly slice across.

Peel 1 lemon and dice, carefully removing all pith and seeds. Squeeze juice from second lemon. Toss parsley, onion and diced lemon. Salt lightly and sprinkle with lemon juice. Toss again.

Serve chilled, either alone or with other salads, or accompanied by a hot first course.

To prepare this soup customarily made for Ramadan, you can also use half soaked chickpeas and half lentils. This will increase the cooking time by 30 minutes. Serve with lemon quarters and fresh cilantro.

[hearty lentil (harira)]

Serves 6
Prep time: 15 minutes
Cooking time: 1½ hours
Standing time: 1 hour

¾ pound boneless
  shoulder of lamb
  with fat removed
1 large onion
1 cross-sectional slice
  ginger root
¾ cup lentils
  (about 5 ounces)
3 sprigs fresh parsley
1 stalk celery
1 stick cinnamon
½ teaspoon turmeric
½ teaspoon paprika
½ teaspoon cumin
Salt and pepper
3 tablespoons flour
1 tablespoon lemon juice
½ cup rice
4 sprigs fresh cilantro
¾ cup tomato sauce
1 tablespoon butter

Dice meat finely. Peel and chop onion. Peel ginger root, slice and grate. In a stockpot, combine onion, ginger, meat, lentils, parsley sprigs, celery stalk, cinnamon stick, turmeric, paprika and cumin. Add 3 quarts water and bring to a boil. Season with salt and pepper, cover and simmer for 1 hour over medium heat.

In the meantime, mix flour with ½ cup water. Add lemon juice and set aside for at least 1 hour at room temperature.

Rinse rice in cold water, add to stockpot and simmer for an additional 20 minutes.

Wash cilantro, dry and chop leaves. Add chopped cilantro to soup along with tomato sauce and butter. Stir and simmer for 5 minutes.

Remove parsley sprigs, celery stalk and cinnamon stick. Remove stockpot from heat and add flour, mixing carefully. Bring to a boil again and then cook for an additional 5 minutes, stirring several times. Season with salt and pepper. Garnish with chopped cilantro, if desired.

Serve this soup piping hot.

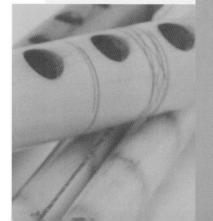

[artichoke and orange salad]

Serves 4
Prep time: 15 minutes
Cooking time: 1 hour

6 frozen artichoke hearts
3 oranges
1 lemon
3 tablespoons olive oil, divided
1 clove garlic
Salt and pepper

In a saucepan, bring a large quantity of water to a boil, add artichoke hearts and boil for 10 minutes.

In the meantime, peel 2 oranges, carefully removing all pith, cut into thick round slices, remove seeds and cut each slice into quarters. Squeeze juice from lemon and the remaining orange. Peel and chop garlic clove.

In a sauté pan, bring ¼ cup water to a boil with lemon and orange juice. Add 1 tablespoon of the oil, chopped garlic and orange pieces. Season with salt and pepper.

Drain artichoke hearts thoroughly, cut into quarters and add to the sauté pan. Cover and simmer for 50 minutes over low heat.

Let cool completely, then sprinkle with the remaining oil. Serve this salad very cold. Garnish with lemon or orange zest, if desired.

[bell pepper preserves]

Serves 6
Prep time: 30 minutes
Cooking time: 45 minutes

3 red bell peppers
3 yellow bell peppers
2 pounds tomatoes
4 cloves garlic
1 bunch fresh parsley
1 bunch fresh cilantro
4 tablespoons olive oil
2 tablespoons mild paprika
1 teaspoon cumin
Chili powder
Salt

Grill bell peppers under the broiler as close to the element as possible, turning as soon as the tops blacken. When the peels are black on all sides, remove peppers from oven and let cool.

Plunge tomatoes into boiling water for 10 seconds, then cold water, and then peel. Remove seeds and chop flesh. Peel garlic cloves and squeeze through a garlic press. Wash parsley and cilantro, and pat dry and chop.

Peel bell peppers, remove stems, seeds and white filaments and dice flesh.

In a frying pan, heat oil. Sauté bell peppers for several minutes while stirring constantly and add tomatoes, garlic, chopped herbs, paprika and cumin. Season to taste with several pinches of chili powder. Add salt. Simmer for 30 minutes, stirring often, until vegetable water has completely evaporated. When done cooking, the bell peppers should look like preserves. Serve hot with grilled meat or cold as a first course.

Chachouka is similar to ratatouille, which means that there is no end to the possible variations. You can make it with eggplant, onions (often combined with chickpeas and small fava beans), tomatoes and fresh chile peppers, potatoes, artichokes, peas, pumpkin, carrots, cauliflower, winter squash, etc.

سكر النمر

ب من السكر

Preheat oven to 350°F. Wash and dry tomatoes, cut in half and remove seeds. Arrange on an oiled baking dish, cut side down, and cook for 20 minutes in the oven.

Turn tomatoes. Season with salt and pepper. Sprinkle with sugar and olive oil and return to the oven; cook for about 1 hour. Carefully remove tomatoes from the dish with a spatula and arrange on another dish. Let cool.

Serve these tomatoes cold as a first course with other salads.

Prep time: 10 minutes
Cooking time:
1 hour 20 minutes

2 pounds medium-
  sized tomatoes
  (of equal size)
Oil for baking dish
Salt and pepper
2 tablespoons
  superfine sugar
¼ cup olive oil

[caramelized tomatoes]

Mediterranean cuisine as a whole tends to bring out the

best in vegetables—and Moroccan cuisine is no exception.

Specialties involving vegetables preserved in olive oil are

numerous. Eggplants and tomatoes are ever present and

garlic is essential. These salads can be served chilled,

but also at room temperature to enhance the flavor of the

vegetables and aromatics and, it is supposed to make

them easier to digest.

[eggplant salad]

Place eggplants under the broiler and broil for 20–25 minutes until the peels are almost charred, turning them once halfway through. Let cool.

Plunge tomatoes into boiling water for 10 seconds, then into cold water and peel. Cut into quarters, remove seeds and chop flesh with a knife. Peel garlic cloves and squeeze through a garlic press.

Remove stem and seeds from chile pepper, (if using) while wearing gloves or under cold running water. Chop finely.

Remove stems and slit open eggplants. Remove flesh with a spoon and chop.

In a sauté pan, heat oil. Sauté eggplant, garlic, tomatoes and chile pepper (if any) for 5 minutes. Add cumin, paprika, salt, pepper and lemon juice. Stir and simmer for 20–25 minutes, stirring often, until the water has evaporated. Sprinkle with chopped cilantro. Serve hot or cold.

Serves 6
Prep and cooking time:
1 hour

3 large eggplants
2 tomatoes
6 cloves garlic
1 small hot chile pepper
 (optional)
4 tablespoons olive oil
½ teaspoon cumin
1 teaspoon paprika
Salt and pepper
2 tablespoons lemon juice
1 tablespoon chopped
 fresh cilantro

[roast vegetable salad]

Wash tomatoes, bell peppers and chile pepper. Place on a large dish and slide under the broiler as close to the element as possible. Turn when the skin is almost charred. Remove each one, as it becomes black on all sides and let cool.

Peel tomatoes, remove seeds and dice. Peel bell peppers and chile peppers. Remove stems, seeds and white filaments, and cut into cross sections or dice.

Peel and chop garlic. Combine vegetables, garlic, salt and pepper. Stir in oil, lemon juice and cumin, and refrigerate for at least 1 hour. Sprinkle with chopped parsley.

Serves 4
Prep and cooking time:
20 minutes
Refrigeration time: 1 hour

4 tomatoes
2 red bell peppers
1 yellow bell pepper
1–2 hot green chile peppers
3 cloves garlic
Salt and pepper
3 tablespoons olive oil
1 tablespoon lemon juice
1 pinch cumin
4 sprigs fresh parsley,
 chopped

Serves 4
Prep and cooking time:
20 minutes*

2 bell peppers
2 lemons preserved in brine
  (see page 40)
1 clove garlic
1 pinch cumin
2 tablespoons lemon juice
1 tablespoon olive oil

[preserved lemon and bell pepper salad]

Grill bell peppers under the broiler as close to the element as possible, turning each one as the peel becomes charred. When the peels are black on all sides, remove bell peppers from the oven and let cool.

Finish cutting the preserved lemons into quarters. Peel garlic clove and mince. Combine garlic with cumin, lemon juice and olive oil.

When the bell peppers are cool, peel them. Remove the stems, seeds and white filaments and cut into strips. Arrange bell peppers and lemon quarters on a serving dish and sprinkle with the sauce. Serve very cold.

*Lemons preserved in brine (see page 40) take 3 days, plus 1 month to pickle. They may be purchased at specialty stores or, perhaps, a Moroccan or Middle Eastern restaurant will sell them.

tagines

tagines

sealed-in flavors

A "tagine" is a large, glazed, earthenware cooking pot with a tall, conical lid.

It can be used to prepare the marvelous simmered dishes of the same name,

but is not absolutely essential. You can also use a cast-iron or earthenware cas-

serole, being careful to follow the directions for cooking times and the order in

which ingredients are added.

[harissa]

Makes 1 small jar
Prep time: 25 minutes
Soaking time: 2 hours

2 ounces dried
  chile peppers
5 cloves garlic
1 tablespoon
  coriander seeds
1 tablespoon cumin seeds
Salt
1 tablespoon vinegar
3 tablespoons olive oil,
  divided

Place peppers in a bowl of cold water and soak for 2 hours.

Drain peppers. Remove stems and seeds, while protecting your hands with rubber gloves or work under cold water.

Peel and chop garlic cloves. Combine chile peppers, coriander, cumin and garlic and crush until a paste is formed. Add salt, vinegar and 2 tablespoons of the olive oil.

Pack harissa into a small glass jar, pour the remaining oil over the top, cover and keep in the refrigerator for up to 1 month, being careful to cover it with a layer of oil after each use.

[lamb tagine with prunes]

Peel and chop onion. In a tagine or casserole, combine onion, meat, cinnamon stick, turmeric, ground ginger, olive oil, salt and pepper. Add just enough water to cover the meat, bring to a boil and then reduce heat and simmer for 1½ hours, partially covered.

Add prunes and sprinkle with honey and cinnamon. Simmer for at least 15 more minutes until the meat is nice and tender.

In a small, ungreased frying pan, brown sesame seeds and sprinkle over the dish. Serve very hot.

Following these same general guidelines, you can prepare a number of other variants.

For a date tagine, substitute ½ pound fresh dates for the prunes.

To prepare a pear tagine, begin by cooking the meat as described above and add the honey and cinnamon for 15 minutes before it's done. Peel 6 pears, cut them in half, remove cores and seeds, and sauté in a frying pan with butter until they are slightly caramelized. Arrange them on top of the meat just before serving.

For an apple tagine, follow the same procedure as for pears, browning the apples separately in butter.

Instead of sesame seeds, you can use whole skinned almonds toasted in butter, or use a mixture of sesame seeds and almonds.

You can also prepare these recipes using chicken. In this case, reduce the cooking time to 1 hour.

Serves 6
Prep time: 15 minutes
Cooking time: 1½ hours

1 large onion
3½ pounds lamb shoulder (with bone)
1 stick cinnamon
½ teaspoon turmeric
2 pinches ground ginger
3 tablespoons olive oil
Salt and pepper
1 pound prunes
3 tablespoons honey
1 teaspoon ground cinnamon
1 tablespoon sesame seeds

[lamb and
eggplant tagine]

Peel onions and cut into thin cross sections. Peel and chop garlic cloves. Crush ginger. Wash parsley and cilantro, pat thoroughly dry and chop leaves.

In a tagine or casserole, combine onion, garlic, ginger, turmeric, cumin, parsley and cilantro. Add oil and butter and heat slowly, while stirring carefully. Add lamb pieces and stir until they are completely coated with sauce. Season with salt and pepper. Add just enough water to cover and bring to a boil. Cover the pot three-quarters of the way, reduce heat and simmer for 1 hour.

In the meantime, wash eggplants, remove stems and cut into pieces. Set aside in salted water, while tagine is simmering.

Drain eggplants thoroughly. Add to casserole, sprinkling them with lemon juice and salting lightly. Simmer for another 30 minutes. If there appears to be too much liquid, reduce it by cooking over high heat until thickened. Serve this tagine piping hot.

You can also cut the eggplants into round slices and brown them separately in a little hot oil before mashing them with a fork and place them on top of the meat just before serving.

Serves 4
Prep time: 20 minutes
Cooking time:
1 hour 40 minutes

2 onions
2 cloves garlic
1 cross-sectional slice
   ginger root
2 sprigs fresh parsley
2 sprigs fresh cilantro
½ teaspoon turmeric
3 pinches ground cumin
2 tablespoons oil
4 teaspoons butter
2 pounds lamb shoulder
   (cut into pieces)
Salt and pepper
2 pounds eggplants
2 tablespoons lemon juice

Serves 4
Prep time: 25 minutes
Cooking time: 50 minutes

2 ounces skinned almonds
5 tablespoons butter,
  divided
⅓ cup couscous
1 teaspoon ras el hanout
  (see glossary for
  description)*
Salt
4 packaged pigeons
1 onion
2 cloves garlic
2 pinches ginger
1 stick cinnamon
1 jar saffron
Pepper

[pigeons stuffed with almonds]

In a frying pan, brown almonds in 1 tablespoon of the butter. Place in a blender or food processor and process just long enough to chop them coarsely.

Combine chopped almonds, couscous, 1 tablespoon of the butter (at room temperature), ras el hanout and salt, and stuff pigeons with this mixture. Close opening with a small skewer, or with a needle and thread.

Peel onion and garlic cloves and chop. In a tagine or small casserole, combine onion, garlic, ground ginger, cinnamon and saffron. Place stuffed pigeons on top of this bed of spices and aromatics, and season with salt and pepper. Add enough water to cover halfway and slowly bring to a boil.

Add the remaining butter, cover and simmer gently for 45 minutes until the pigeons are very tender.

Remove cover and reduce liquid until it is sufficiently creamy. Coat and brown the pigeons in the thick sauce that forms. Serve very hot.

*A simple version of this spice blend made from spices readily available in grocery stores follows. However, if you are able to find the real item from a specialty store or Moroccan or Middle Eastern restaurant, it would be preferable.

Simplified Ras el Hanout, made from ground spices:
1 teaspoon each black pepper, ginger;
½ teaspoon each cumin, cinnamon, corriander, allspice, cardamom;
¼ teaspoon each nutmeg, turmeric;
⅛ teaspoon cloves, cayenne pepper

[fish marinade]

Wash cilantro, dry thoroughly and remove leaves. Peel garlic and cut cloves in half. Squeeze juice from lemons. Place cilantro leaves and garlic in a blender or food processor. Add salt and 4 tablespoons water, and purée.

Pour contents of blender or food processor into a shallow dish. Add cumin, paprika (or mild chili powder), and hot chili powder, lemon juice and oil. Mix thoroughly.

For 1 fish
(about 3–4 pounds)
Prep time: 10 minutes

1 small bunch fresh cilantro
5 cloves garlic
2 lemons
Salt
1 teaspoon ground cumin
½ teaspoon paprika or
  mild chili powder
1 pinch hot chili powder
2 tablespoons oil

[chicken tagine with lemons and olives]

Serves 5–6
Prep time: 20 minutes
Cooking time: 1 hour

1 chicken (about
   3½ pounds)
1 onion
4 cloves garlic
3 sprigs fresh parsley
3 sprigs fresh cilantro
4 tablespoons olive oil
3 tablespoons butter
2 pinches ginger
1 teaspoon turmeric
½ teaspoon ground
   cinnamon
Salt and pepper
2 preserved lemons
   (see page 40)
⅔ cup olives (purple
   olives, if possible)

Cut up chicken. Peel onion and garlic and chop separately. Wash parsley and cilantro and chop finely.

In a tagine or casserole, heat oil. Add butter. When it becomes foamy, add onion, ginger, turmeric, cinnamon and salt. Season generously with pepper and stir.

Place chicken pieces in casserole and turn them to coat with the sauce, then brown on all sides over high heat.

Add chopped garlic, parsley and cilantro. Add ¾ cup water, bring to a boil, cover and simmer for 50 minutes over low heat. Remove chicken and keep warm.

Reduce the sauce. Cut lemons into quarters and add to sauce along with olives and chicken pieces. Heat slowly and serve very hot.

[lamb kebabs]

Serves 4
Prep time: 15 minutes
Cooking time: 1½–2 hours

1½ pounds boneless
    mutton or lamb steaks
    from the leg
1 onion
2 cloves garlic
3 sprigs fresh parsley
½ teaspoon ground cumin
2-3 pinches hot chili powder
4 tablespoons butter
1–2 preserved lemons
    (see page 40)
Salt and pepper

Cut meat into cubes of about 1½ inches. Peel and chop onion and garlic cloves. Chop parsley.

In a sauté pan or small stovetop casserole, combine meat pieces with onion, garlic, cumin, chili powder, parsley, butter, salt and pepper. Add just enough water to cover the meat and bring to a boil. Reduce heat, cover and simmer gently for 1½–2 hours until the meat is tender.

When the meat is done, remove the cover and reduce the meat juices until they take on a creamy consistency. Pour meat and its juices into a tagine or shallow serving dish. Garnish with 1 or 2 preserved lemons cut into quarters.

You can serve this tagine just as it is or, when it's done cooking, break 4 eggs into the sauce and let them poach until the whites set.

[lemons preserved in brine]

Prep time: 15 minutes
Soaking time: 4 days
Pickling time:
3 days, plus 1 month

Very ripe organic lemons
Kosher salt

Scrub lemons under warm water. Soak 4 days in cold water, changing water once a day.

Cut lemons lengthwise as though to quarter them, but not cutting all the way through, leaving quarters joined at the center and each end. Insert 2 pinches kosher salt into each cut, close up the lemons and pack them as tightly as possible into sterilized, dry jars. Add 1 tablespoon kosher salt. Close jars and let pickle for 3 days.

If the lemons are not submerged in their own juice at the end of three days, fill the jars to the top with boiling water. Close and let pickle set for 1 month in a dark place.

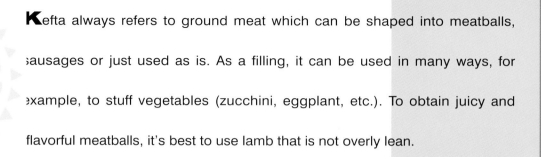

Kefta always refers to ground meat which can be shaped into meatballs, sausages or just used as is. As a filling, it can be used in many ways, for example, to stuff vegetables (zucchini, eggplant, etc.). To obtain juicy and flavorful meatballs, it's best to use lamb that is not overly lean.

[meatball tagine with tomatoes]

Prepare the meatballs: Mix all the ingredients together with your hands, season with salt and pepper and set aside for at least 30 minutes.

In the meantime, peel onions and garlic cloves and mince. In a tagine or sauté pan, melt butter and sauté onions and garlic for 5 minutes over low heat while stirring. Add tomatoes and their juice and mash them with a fork. Add turmeric, sugar and chili powder. Salt lightly and season with pepper. Simmer for 30 minutes uncovered.

Roll small amounts of ground meat into meatballs of about 1 inch. Place meatballs in tomato sauce, partially cover and simmer gently for 20 minutes. When done, the sauce should be fairly thick. If it is not, remove all the meatballs with a skimmer, reduce the sauce over high heat and return the meatballs to the sauce for several seconds to reheat them. Serve hot.

You can serve this tagine just as it is or, at the last minute, break 4 eggs into the sauce and poach them.

This recipe can also be prepared with beef that is slightly fatty. You can also add 1 handful skinned almonds and/or 8 pitted dates to the sauce. This dish can be prepared ahead of time. Just reheat it slowly before serving.

Serves 4–5
Prep time: 30 minutes
Standing time: 30 minutes
Cooking time: 1 hour

For the meatballs:
1 pound ground lamb
1 teaspoon ras el hanout
  (see page 37)
½ teaspoon ground cumin
1 teaspoon paprika or
  mild chili powder
2 tablespoons chopped
  fresh parsley
2 tablespoons chopped
  fresh cilantro
1 pinch hot chili powder
Salt and pepper

For the tagine:
2 onions
4 cloves garlic
4 tablespoons butter
2 large cans
  peeled tomatoes
  (28 ounces each)
½ teaspoon turmeric
1 teaspoon sugar
2–3 pinches hot
  chili powder

[fish tagine]

Serves 4–6
Prep time: 15 minutes
Marinating time:
at least 2 hours
Cooking time: 25 minutes

Fish marinade
(see page 38)
1 sea bass or grouper,
thoroughly scaled
(about 3½ pounds)
1 cross-sectional slice
ginger root
1 jar saffron
2 tablespoons oil
12 olives
1–2 preserved lemons
(see page 40)

Prepare the fish marinade (see page 38).

Cut fish into slices about 1½ inches thick, wash and pat dry thoroughly with paper towels. Place fish pieces in a shallow dish containing the marinade, and turn them so that they are completely coated, cover and marinate for at least 2 hours in a cool place.

Peel ginger slice and grate. Combine ginger with saffron, oil and marinade, pour into a casserole and simmer for 10 minutes over low heat.

Drain fish pieces, transfer to the casserole, cover and simmer for 8 minutes without bringing to a boil. Turn fish pieces using a wide spatula and simmer for several more minutes.

Arrange fish slices on a serving dish, and surround with olives and preserved lemons cut into quarters. If there is too much liquid, reduce the sauce before pouring it over the fish. Serve right away!

[lamb tagine with onions]

Combine meat with ½ tablespoon of the cinnamon, turmeric, salt and pepper.

In a tagine or casserole, heat 3 tablespoons of the olive oil. When it is very hot, sauté spiced meat for 10 minutes, stirring with a wooden spoon. Pour ¾ cup hot water over the meat, cover and simmer for 1 hour.

In the meantime, peel all the onions, quarter, then thinly slice across. In a frying pan, heat the remaining oil and sauté onions until golden. Then sprinkle them with sugar and the remaining cinnamon and stir well.

Pour onions onto the meat, partially cover, and simmer for about 45 minutes until the meat is tender.

If too much liquid remains when the tagine is done, remove the cover and let the liquid evaporate for a few moments. Serve this tagine piping hot.

Serves 6
Prep time: 30 minutes
Cooking time: 2 hours

3½ pounds lamb shoulder
  (with bones) or neck of
  lamb, cut into chunks
1 tablespoon ground
  cinnamon, divided
1 teaspoon turmeric
Salt and pepper
5 tablespoons olive oil,
  divided
2 pounds onions
2 tablespoons sugar

[quail with grapes]

Peel onions and chop very finely. Peel garlic clove and squeeze through a garlic press. Season quail inside and out with salt and pepper.

In a small casserole, melt 4 tablespoons of the butter. Add onions and garlic, season generously with salt and pepper and stir. Place quails on this bed, pour on ½ cup of water, partially cover, and simmer for 30 minutes over medium heat, turning birds at the halfway point. Then uncover the casserole completely and reduce quail juices.

In the meantime, peel grapes and remove seeds. In a frying pan, melt the remaining butter, add grapes, stir and simmer for 5 minutes over low heat.

Add crème fraîche to the casserole, stir and simmer for several minutes. Season to taste.

Arrange quails and grapes on a serving dish and pour the sauce over the top. Serve hot.

Serves 6
Prep time: 30 minutes
Cooking time: 45 minutes

2 onions
1 clove garlic
6 large quail, cleaned
  (not barded)
Salt and pepper
6 tablespoons butter,
  divided
Salt and pepper
2 pounds white grapes
¼ cup crème fraîche
Salt and pepper

[spiced rabbit]

Peel onions and garlic cloves and mince. Wash parsley and cilantro, dry and chop. In a casserole, combine oil, onions, garlic, chopped herbs, cinnamon and the remaining spices. Season with salt and pepper, and mix thoroughly.

Season rabbit pieces with salt and pepper. Place them (all except the liver) in the casserole, pour 1¼ cups water over the top and slowly bring to a boil.

Cover casserole three-quarters of the way, reduce heat and simmer for at least 1 hour. Add the liver 10 minutes before the rabbit is done. If too much liquid remains, reduce the sauce. Serve very hot.

Serves 4–6
Prep time: 10 minutes
Cooking time: 1½ hours

2 onions
4 cloves garlic
3 sprigs fresh parsley
3 sprigs fresh cilantro
4 tablespoons oil
1 stick cinnamon
1 tablespoon ras el hanout
3 pinches ground ginger
3 pinches ground cumin
3 pinches freshly
  grated nutmeg
Salt and pepper
1 large rabbit cut into
  pieces, rabbit liver

Serves 4–5
Prep time: 15 minutes
Cooking time: 1½ hours

3 handfuls raisins
⅓ cup couscous
2 teaspoons ras el hanout
1 teaspoon ground
  cinnamon
3 tablespoons honey,
  divided
Salt and pepper
4 teaspoons salted butter
1 chicken (about 3 pounds)
1 chopped onion
1 cross-sectional slice
  ginger root
1 stick cinnamon
2 tablespoons oil
2 tablespoons sweet butter
1 teaspoon turmeric

[chicken stuffed with couscous and raisins]

Soak raisins in a bowl of warm water. Sprinkle couscous with 2 tablespoons water. Combine raisins with couscous, ground spices, 1 tablespoon of the honey, salt, pepper and salted butter. Stuff chicken, and sew it closed.

In a tagine or casserole, combine onion, ginger, cinnamon stick, salt, pepper and oil. Place the chicken on top, spread sweet butter over it, cover halfway with water and bring to a boil. Cover and simmer for about 1½ hours.

Sprinkle chicken with turmeric and pour the remaining honey over the top. Turn it over several times in the thick sauce, letting it brown. Serve very hot.

couscous & brochettes

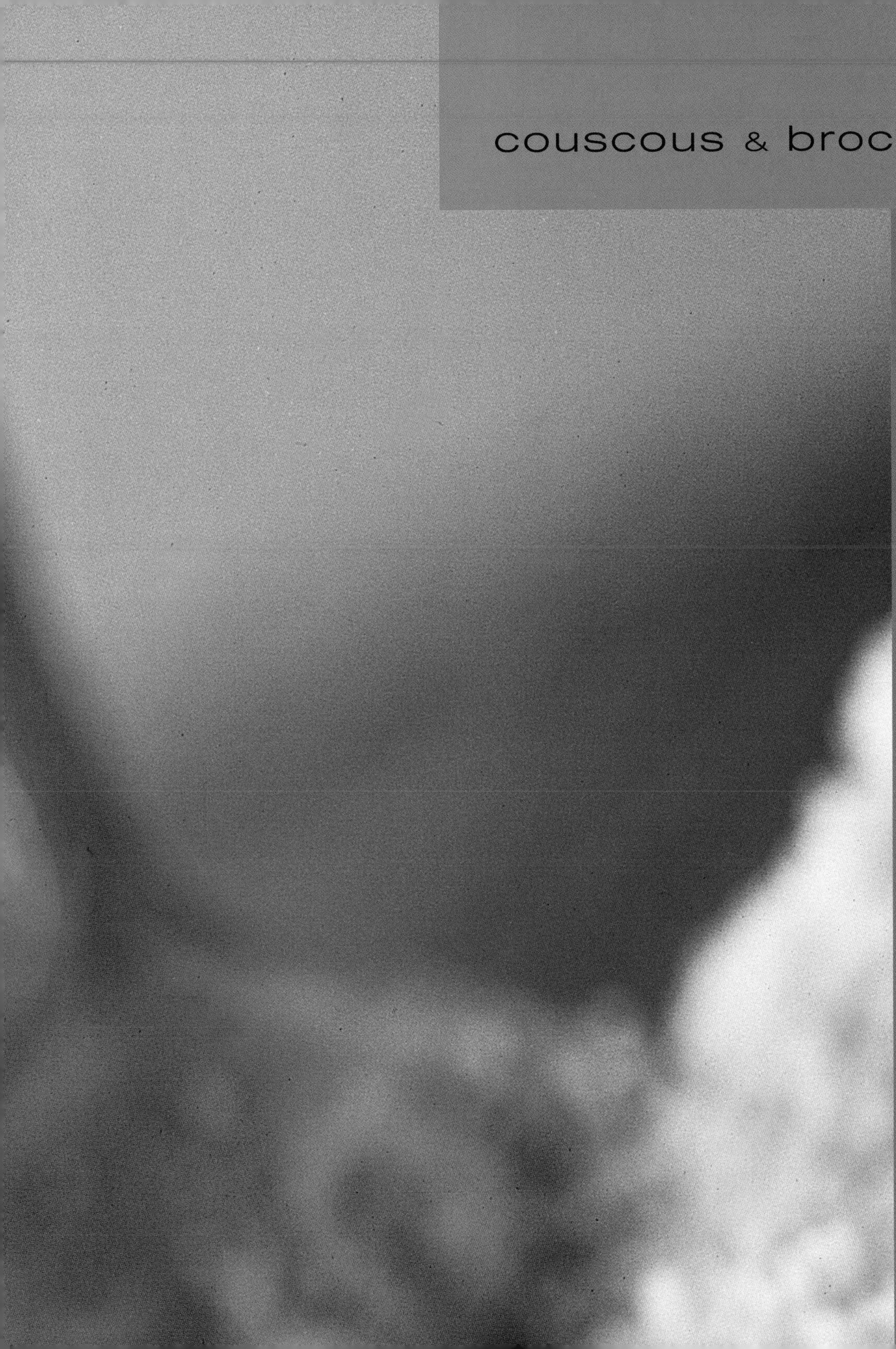

couscous & brochettes

a universal dish

How much do we really know about couscous? Because it is so common, we tend to forget its truly miraculous nature. It is the perfect, nutritionally balanced meal that never becomes boring. Between the different meats, fishes, vegetables and spices that can be used, the variations are endless. We can serve it alone, soaked with stock, highly spiced or mild, and sweet. We can use it to stuff poultry or offer it as dessert.

[beef kebab]

Serves 4
Prep time: 15 minutes
Marinating time: 3–4 hours
Cooking time: 5–8 minutes

1¼ pounds beef sirloin
2 onions
3 sprigs fresh parsley
Salt and pepper

With a very sharp knife, cut away the layer of fat from the sirloin, then cut meat into cubes of about 1 inch.

Peel onions and mince. Wash parsley, pat dry with paper towels and chop leaves.

Place meat, onions and parsley in a bowl. Season with salt and pepper. Mix together for a long time with your hands, then set aside to marinate for 3–4 hours in a cool place.

A few minutes before cooking, thread meat pieces onto 4 skewers and sear on a very hot cast-iron grill, under the oven broiler or on a barbecue grill. Cook skewers for 5–8 minutes, depending on how done you want them, turning at regular intervals.

Moroccans alternate pieces of fat with cubes of meat, which you can also do if you use a fillet.

[fish stuffed with spinach]

Prepare the fish marinade (see page 38). Rinse fish and pat dry. Roll in marinade and marinate for 2 hours in a cool place.

Remove stalks from spinach, wash leaves, and steam until very tender. Then drain. Finely dice preserved lemon. Preheat oven to 400°F. Squeeze out spinach thoroughly with your hands and combine with diced preserved lemon and sugar. Stuff fish with this mixture, and sew or tie it shut.

Pour half the oil onto a long dish and lay the fish on top of it. Pour the remaining oil over the top along with 3 tablespoons water, salt and pepper. Dissolve turmeric and 3 pinches salt in 2 tablespoons water and the lemon juice, and pour over the fish. Bake for 35–40 minutes in the oven.

In the meantime, prepare the couscous according to package directions, or traditional method (see page 60), mixing in the oil and butter.

Another way to prepare this dish is by stuffing the fish with dates and almonds. In this case, brown 1 large chopped onion in 1 tablespoon oil. Toast ¼ cup skinned almonds separately without using any fat. Combine onion, almonds and ½ cup pitted dates. Add 2 tablespoons unsalted butter, 1 tablespoon lemon juice, 2 teaspoons nutmeg, 2 jars saffron, 1 pinch ground coriander, salt and a generous amount of pepper. Stuff the fish with this mixture and bake in the oven. Serve surrounded by toasted slivered almonds.

Serves 4–5
Prep time: 20 minutes
Marinating time: 2 hours
Cooking time:
35–40 minutes

Fish marinade
 (see page 38)
1 grouper or sea bass,
 thoroughly scaled and
 cleaned (3½ pounds)
1 pound fresh spinach
1 lemon preserved in brine
 (see page 40)
½ teaspoon sugar
4 tablespoons oil, divided
Salt and pepper
½ teaspoon turmeric
4 tablespoons lemon juice

For the couscous:
1 package couscous
 (12 ounces), or 2½ cups
 couscous (see page 60)
3 tablespoons oil
5 tablespoons butter

[squab couscous]

Combine honey, 2 teaspoons of the cinnamon, saffron, salt and pepper, and coat squabs with this mixture.

Peel onions and cut into thin cross sections. Place onion slices in a steamer and add cinnamon stick, whole cloves, ground ginger, salt and a generous amount of pepper. Place the squabs on this bed of aromatics and spices. Add 6 cups water, bring to a boil and then simmer for 30 minutes.

Prepare the couscous according to package directions, or use traditional method (see page 60), mixing in the oil and butter. Soak raisins in a little warm water to which you have added the orange blossom water. Wash apricots.

After 30 minutes, continue simmering squabs over low heat but remove onions with a skimmer and transfer to a saucepan, containing 1 ladle pigeon stock, 4 teaspoons butter, sugar and 1 teaspoon cinnamon. Sauté over medium heat until they are thoroughly candied. Drain raisins. Add raisins and apricots to the onions, stir and let liquid evaporate completely.

In a frying pan, heat oil and brown almonds. Dry on a paper towel.

On a large shallow serving dish, arrange the following ingredients in successive layers in a pyramid formation: couscous, onion-raisin-apricot mixture, squabs cut in half, sauce, couscous, etc., finishing with a layer of couscous. Dust with the remaining teaspoon of cinnamon and sprinkle with fried almonds.

Serves 4
Prep time: 30 minutes
Cooking time 45 minutes

2 tablespoons honey
4 teaspoons ground
  cinnamon, divided
1 jar saffron
Salt
Pepper
4 cleaned squabs
2 pounds onions
1 stick cinnamon
4 whole cloves
½ teaspoon ground ginger

For the couscous:
1 package couscous
  (12 ounces), or 2½ cups
  couscous (see page 60)
3 tablespoons oil
4 tablespoons butter
¾ cup raisins
1 tablespoon orange
  blossom water
15 dried apricots
4 teaspoons butter
1 tablespoon sugar
1 tablespoon oil
½ cup skinned almonds

Serves 4
Prep time: 20 minutes
Marinating time:
at least 2 hours
Cooking time: 8 minutes

1 onion
2 fresh mint leaves
1 pound ground sirloin
1 teaspoon ras el hanout
½ teaspoon ground cumin
1 teaspoon paprika or mild
  chili powder
2 tablespoons chopped
  fresh parsley
2 tablespoons chopped
  fresh cilantro
1 pinch hot chili powder
Salt and pepper

[kefta brochettes]

Peel onion. Finely chop onion and mint leaves. Combine ground meat, mint leaves, onion, and all the spices and chopped herbs, and chili powder, salt and pepper and knead everything together with your hands. Marinate for at least 2 hours in the refrigerator.

Wet your hands and divide the meat preparation into portions the size of an egg. Roll them between your palms and mold each one around a skewer, shaping it into a small sausage. If the skewers are long enough, place 3 meatballs on each one.

Place the brochettes on a barbecue grill or under a broiler and cook for about 8 minutes, turning them at regular intervals. Serve with an assortment of salads.

You can prepare similar brochettes made of lamb.

[stuffed leg of lamb]

Serves 6
Prep time: 15 minutes
Cooking time: 1 hour

½ cup couscous
1 tablespoon
  skinned almonds
1 small onion
2 tablespoons butter,
  divided
1 tablespoon raisins
1 pinch ground ginger
1 jar saffron
Salt and pepper
1 deboned leg of lamb
  (about 4½ pounds)

Sprinkle 3 tablespoons salted water over couscous. Chop almonds coarsely. Peel and grate onion.

When couscous has absorbed all the water, add 1 tablespoon of the butter cut into small bits, almonds, raisins, onion, ginger and saffron. Season with salt and pepper. Knead together well and use to stuff leg of lamb. Tie lamb closed as you would a roast.

Preheat oven to 425°F. Smear remaining butter on leg of lamb. Place on a rack over a roasting pan containing 3 tablespoons water and bake for 1 hour in the oven.

[onion and raisin couscous]

In a large pan, combine 1 heaping tablespoon of the onions, meat, butter, turmeric, ras el hanout, salt, pepper and 2 quarts water. Bring to a boil and simmer for 1 hour.

Prepare the couscous according to package directions, or traditional method (see page 60), mixing in the oil and butter. Drain and rinse chickpeas.

After cooking the meat for 1 hour, add raisins, remaining onions and chickpeas, and simmer for another 30 minutes. If the sauce is not creamy enough, reduce. Serve piping hot with couscous.

Serves 4
Prep time: 20 minutes
Cooking time: 1½ hours

1½ pounds frozen chopped
   onions, divided
2 pounds lamb with the
   bone, cut into chunks
4 tablespoons butter
1 teaspoon turmeric
2 tablespoon ras el hanout
   (see page 37)
Salt and pepper

For the couscous:
1 package couscous
   (12 ounces), or 2 cups
   couscous (see page 60)
3 tablespoons oil
4 tablespoons butter
1 can chickpeas (garbanzo
   beans; 15½ ounces)
2 cups raisins

Serves 4
Prep and cooking time:
20 minutes
Marinating time:
at least 1 hour

1¾ pounds swordfish
 or some kind of firm
 white fish
Fish marinade
 (see page 38)
3 sprigs fresh parsley

[fish brochettes]

Rinse fish, dry carefully with paper towels and cut into cubes.

Prepare fish marinade. Wash parsley, dry, and chop leaves and add to marinade.

Mix fish cubes with marinade and marinate for at least 1 hour in the refrigerator.

Remove fish pieces from marinade and thread onto 4 skewers. Grill on a hot cast-iron grill, under the broiler or on a barbecue grill, turning as often as needed for grilling.

Serve brochettes hot with steamed potatoes and a crisp salad.

[fish stuffed with couscous]

Sprinkle couscous with ¼ cup boiling salted water and leave to soak. Brown almonds in 1 tablespoon of the butter and chop coarsely.

Melt the remaining butter. When couscous has absorbed all the water, separate the grains with your fingers and add melted butter, half the raisins, almonds, 2 tablespoons of the sugar, half the cinnamon, ginger and turmeric. Mix carefully.

Rinse fish, dry thoroughly with paper towels and stuff (including the head) with seasoned couscous.

Preheat oven to 350°F.

In a saucepan, combine ½ cup water, 3 tablespoons of the oil, the remaining cinnamon, sugar, raisins and 1 pinch salt and bring to a boil. Simmer for 5 minutes. Place fish in a long, baking dish greased with the remaining oil. Cover with contents of saucepan and bake for 40 minutes in the oven.

Serves 5–6
Prep time: 20 minutes
Cooking time: 40 minutes

½ cup couscous
3 tablespoons skinned almonds
2 tablespoons butter, divided
½ cup raisins, divided
⅓ cup sugar, divided
1 teaspoon ground cinnamon, divided
2 pinches ground ginger
3 pinches turmeric
1 sea bass or grouper (about 4½ pounds), cleaned through the gills (i.e. all the innards pulled out through the gills without cutting open the fish)
4 tablespoons oil, divided
Salt

[preparing couscous, traditional couscoussier method*]

Pour cold water over couscous and spread it out over a large dish, separating the grains. Transfer to the upper section of a couscoussier and place this section on top of the pot in which the meat and vegetables are cooking, tying a dish towel around the seam between the two sections. Do not cover.

When you see large amounts of steam rising through the couscous, pour it into a large dish. Sprinkle with oil and ¾ cup water, while mixing it with your hands.

When all the liquid has been absorbed, return the couscous to the upper section of the couscoussier. Simmer uncovered until large amounts of steam are again rising. Pour into a dish, season with salt and mix in butter cut into bits.

*Couscous may also be purchased in a 12-ounce package, which serves 6 people. Prepare according to directions on package.

Serves 6
Prep and cooking time: 1 hour

3 cups couscous (20 ounces)
4 tablespoons oil
Salt
½ cup butter

Grapes and onions seasoned with cinnamon lend a unique sweetness to this traditional couscous dish, which is always a hit in both winter and summer. The almonds give it a hint of decadence and sophistication.

[lamb and chicken couscous with vegetables]

Scrape carrots, and cut carrots and zucchini into chunks. Remove stems, seeds and white filaments from bell peppers and dice flesh. Peel turnips and cut up. Peel onions and cut into thin cross sections. Chop cilantro.

In a large pan, heat 2 tablespoons of the oil. Sauté lamb, chicken and onions. Add salt, pepper, cilantro, tomato sauce, ras el hanout, turmeric and whole cloves. Cover with a generous amount of cold water, bring to a boil and simmer for 45 minutes.

Soak raisins in warm water to which you have added the orange blossom water. Prepare the couscous (see page 60), mixing butter and oil.

After 45 minutes, remove onions with a skimmer and place in a colander. To the lamb mixture, add carrots, zucchini, turnips and bell peppers. Simmer for another 45 minutes, adding chickpeas after 30 minutes.

Sauté onions with the butter, sugar and cinnamon until they are candied. Drain raisins, add to onions and let caramelize. Brown almonds in the remaining oil.

Arrange couscous in a ring formation on a serving dish, pour 1 ladle of sauce over it and place meat mixture in the center. Cover with onions and raisins and sprinkle with grilled almonds.

Serves 6
Prep time: 1 hour
Cooking time:
1 hour 30 minutes

3 carrots
3 zucchini
2 red bell peppers
3 small turnips
2 pounds onions
4 sprigs fresh cilantro
3 tablespoons oil, divided
1¾ pounds lamb shoulder, cut into chunks
6 chicken thighs
Salt and pepper
½ cup tomato sauce
2 tablespoons ras el hanout (see page 37)
1 tablespoon turmeric
4 whole coves
1 cup raisins
2 tablespoons orange blossom water

For the couscous:
1 package couscous (12 ounces), or 1¼ pounds couscous (see page 60)
8 tablespoons butter
4 tablespoons oil
4 tablespoons canned chickpeas (garbanzo beans)
2 tablespoons butter
1 tablespoon sugar
1 teaspoon ground cinnamon
½ cup skinned almonds

[seven-vegetable couscous]

Serves 6
Prep time: 30 minutes
Cooking time:
1 hour 45 minutes

5 onions
3 cloves garlic
½ head white cabbage
1½ pounds boneless veal, cut
into chunks
6 tablespoons butter
Salt and pepper
½ teaspoon turmeric
4 carrots
3 turnips
¾ pound fresh pumpkin flesh
2 eggplants
3 tomatoes
1 small fresh chile pepper
2 sprigs fresh cilantro

For the couscous:
1 package couscous
(12 ounces), or
3 cups couscous
(see page 60)
6 tablespoons butter
4 tablespoons oil
½ can chickpeas
(garbanzo beans;
15½ ounces)

Peel onions and garlic and cut both into cross sections. Cut half head of cabbage into quarters. In a large, heavy saucepan, combine meat, the equivalent of 2 onions, garlic, cabbage and butter. Add salt, pepper and turmeric. Pour 3 quarts of water over the top, bring to a boil and simmer for 45 minutes.

Scrape carrots and peel turnips. Cut carrots, turnips, pumpkin, eggplants and tomatoes into chunks. Remove stem and seeds from chile pepper and cut into round slices. Wash cilantro, pat dry and chop leaves. Add carrots, turnips, pumpkin, eggplants, tomatoes, the remaining onions, chile pepper and cilantro to saucepan and simmer for 1 hour.

At the same time, prepare the couscous according to package directions, or traditional method (see page 60), mixing in the oil and butter.

Drain chickpeas and add to saucepan for 15 minutes before it has finished cooking. Season sauce to taste.

Transfer hot cooked couscous to a large round serving dish and pour on as much sauce as it can absorb. Form a well in the center and place meat and vegetables in this well. Pour the remaining sauce into a bowl and serve separately, very hot.

[fish couscous]

Serves 6
Prep time: 25 minutes
Cooking time: 40 minutes

Peel onions and garlic cloves. Cut onions into thin cross sections. Mince garlic. In a stockpot, heat 5 tablespoons of the oil. Braise onions and garlic for 5 minutes without allowing them to brown, stirring constantly. Add tomato sauce, ground cloves, cumin, turmeric, thyme, bay leaf and chile pepper. Season with salt and pepper. Stir, and add ¾ cup water, bring to a boil and simmer for 30 minutes.

In the meantime, prepare the couscous according to package directions, or traditional method (see page 60), mixing in the oil and butter. Set aside.

In a nonstick frying pan, heat the remaining tablespoon of oil. Sauté monkfish for 5 minutes over high heat, then remove from heat and let it excrete

its juices.

Drain monkfish pieces thoroughly, add to sauce along with grouper and simmer gently for 10 minutes.

Pour couscous onto a serving dish in a pyramid formation. Pour 1 ladle of sauce over the top. Drain fish pieces and arrange around the couscous. Remove chile pepper, thyme sprig and bay leaf from the sauce, pour into a bowl and serve very hot.

2 onions
10 cloves garlic
6 tablespoons oil, divided
1¼ cups tomato sauce
3 pinches ground cloves
½ teaspoon ground cumin
½ teaspoon turmeric
1 sprig fresh thyme
1 bay leaf
1 small dried chile pepper
Salt and pepper

For the couscous:
1 package couscous
   (12 ounces), or 3 cups
   couscous (see page 60)
8 tablespoons butter
4 tablespoons oil
1¾ pounds monkfish,
   cut into pieces
1¼ pounds grouper,
   cut into pieces

Prepare the half package of couscous (using half the amount of water etc.) according to package directions, or steam couscous twice with ¼ cup water according to traditional method (see page 60). Sprinkle prepared couscous with butter cut into bits and mix it gently with your hands. Brown almonds in hot oil. Rinse raisins and drain.

Combine couscous that is well coated with butter and the almonds and raisins and sprinkle with sugar, turmeric and cinnamon and ginger. Stuff the bird with this mixture and sew the opening shut.

You can increase or reduce the quantities depending on the size of the bird you want to stuff.

For 1 bird
Prep time: 15 minutes
Cooking time: 45 minutes

½ package couscous
(about 6 ounces), or 1 cup
couscous (see page 60)
1½ tablespoons butter
3 tablespoons skinned
almonds
1 teaspoon oil
⅓ cup raisins
2 tablespoons sugar
3 pinches turmeric
1 teaspoon ground cinnamon
2 pinches ground ginger

[couscous stuffing for poultry]

The city of Fès is known as the birthplace of the most

delicious culinary tradition in Morocco. Enhanced by its

Andalusian, Berber and Jewish heritage, this particular

style is characterized by a mixture of spices that is

harmonious but never excessive. The secret is time. It

originates in an era not altogether past in which wives,

mothers, cooks and servants never counted the hours

spent preparing their feasts.

[steamed chicken]

Wash parsley and cilantro, dry and finely chop leaves. Combine these herbs with all the spices, salt and pepper. Rub the mixture all over the outside of the chicken and place the rest inside. Wrap the chicken in cheesecloth.

Place 2 sprigs thyme in the top section of a couscoussier or a steamer large enough to hold the chicken. Place chicken on top and the remaining 2 sprigs of thyme on top of that. Fill bottom section of couscous or steamer ⅓ of the way full with water. Bring the water to a boil and place upper section on top of bottom section. Cover, reduce heat to obtain a gentle boil and cook for 1 hour and 15 minutes.

When the chicken is done, melt butter in a frying pan and brown chicken on all sides. Serve immediately with small bowls of salt and cumin.

You can also cook a shoulder of lamb in the same way: Rub it with the spice mixture, minus the herbs. When very tender, brown lamb in butter or sprinkle it with chopped cilantro and cook for an additional 15 minutes.

Serves 4–5
Prep time: 20 minutes
Cooking time: 1½ hours

4 sprigs fresh parsley
4 sprigs fresh cilantro
1 teaspoon turmeric
1 teaspoon cumin
1 teaspoon paprika
1½ teaspoons salt
1 teaspoon ground
   black pepper
1 packaged corn-fed
   chicken (about 3 pounds)
4 sprigs fresh thyme
4 tablespoons butter

For serving:
Small dishes of salt
   and cumin

[breakfast couscous with cinnamon]

Brown almonds in hot oil, drain on paper towels and chop coarsely in a blender or food processor.

Prepare couscous according to package directions or, in the top section of a couscoussier, prepare the couscous twice with ½ cup water, and set top section over the bottom section containing 2 quarts of boiling water (see page 60). Fluff prepared couscous well with a fork and then mix in the butter cut into small bits.

Pour half the couscous onto a serving dish, and place almonds on top and then cover with the remaining couscous. Garnish with sugar and cinnamon.

Serve with decorative bowls of milk, and small dishes of powdered sugar and cinnamon.

Serves 6
Prep time: 20 minutes
Cooking time:
about 45 minutes

⅓ cup skinned almonds
1 tablespoon oil
1 package couscous
   (12 ounces), or 2 cups
   fine couscous
⅓ cup butter
1 heaping tablespoon sugar
½ teaspoon ground
   cinnamon

For serving:
1 quart milk
Powdered sugar
Ground cinnamon

Serves 6
Prep time: 15 minutes
Cooking time 1 hour

8 tablespoons
  unsalted butter
3 teaspoons cumin, divided
2 teaspoons mild chili
  powder or paprika, divided
1 deboned unrolled
  lamb shoulder
3 sprigs fresh thyme

[shoulder-of-lamb méchoui]

Combine butter with cumin and chili powder. Spread half this mixture on the inside of the shoulder, roll and tie together. Rub a little of the mixture on the outside. Place the meat on a spit and roast for 1 hour in a rotisserie.

Melt the remaining spiced butter. Bind thyme sprigs together and use this brush to baste meat with melted butter at regular intervals during cooking.

If you have a large oven, you can roast a leg of lamb with the bone, again buttering it at regular intervals.

Méchoui is normally a whole sheep roasted on a spit over an open fire and is suitable only for large numbers of guests. In the city, it's easier to serve smaller groups by roasting a leg of lamb in the oven.

pastillas & briouats

pastillas & briouats

heavenly puff pastry

The pastilla is a monument to Arabian-Andalusian cuisine. Although it takes a

while to prepare, it is not difficult and is well worth the effort. The result will be a

meal so fantastic that your friends will remember it. Pastillas also come in simpli-

fied and smaller-scale versions. While some recipes in this book show round

feuilles de brick—all recipes can be done successfully using rectangular phyllo

dough (see page 116).

[assembling the pastilla]

Lightly butter 6 sheets of phyllo pastry dough on one side only. Arrange them in a baking tin in an overlapping pattern. Stack 2 more sheets (also buttered) one on top of the other in the bottom of the tin. **S**pread half the meat on top of this pastry along with the sauce and almonds. Cover with three buttered sheets of pastry, again in an overlapping pattern, and brush all around with a beaten egg yolk mixed with a little water. Press down slightly to seal the edges.

Cover with the remaining meat, sauce and almonds. Top with 4 buttered sheets of pastry, tucking the edges down into the baking tin. Brush the top with butter.

[pigeon pastilla]

Peel onions. Finely chop onions, parsley and cilantro. Season pigeons with salt and pepper.

In a stovetop casserole or a Dutch oven, heat 2 tablespoons of the oil and 2 tablespoons of the butter and brown pigeons on all sides. Remove pigeons and rapidly sauté onions in the casserole. Add chopped herbs, spices, salt and a generous amount of pepper. Add ⅓ cup water, return pigeons to the casserole, cover and simmer for 1 hour over low heat, turning the birds after ½ hour.

In the meantime, heat the remaining oil in a frying pan. Brown almonds and chop finely. Combine with sugar and cinnamon.

When the pigeons are tender, remove them from the casserole, debone and cut the meat into pieces. Break the eggs and beat them with a fork. Remove the casserole from the heat, add the eggs and stir briskly. Place over low heat and continue stirring several minutes until a creamy sauce is formed.

Preheat oven to 400°F.

Melt the additional butter and pour it into a cup, eliminating the white sediment. Using some of the melted butter, grease a 12-inch cake pan (preferably a false-bottom pan) and assemble the pastilla (see pages 75 and 116).

Place the pastilla in the oven and bake for 30 minutes until it is nice and golden. Remove from the tin, sprinkle lightly with powdered sugar and decorate with a little cinnamon using a stencil.

Serves 6
Prep time: 1 hour
Cooking time: 2 hours

1¼ pounds onions
1 bunch Italian parsley
6 sprigs fresh cilantro
4 cleaned pigeons
Salt and pepper
3 tablespoons oil, divided
2 tablespoons butter
2 tablespoons ras el hanout
2 jars saffron
⅔ cup skinned almonds
3 tablespoons sugar
2 teaspoons ground cinnamon
5 eggs

For assembling the pastilla:
8 tablespoons butter
 (1 stick), additional
15 sheets brick pastry or
 phyllo pastry dough
1 egg yolk, beaten and
 mixed with a little water
Powdered sugar
 for sprinkling
Ground cinnamon
 for decoration

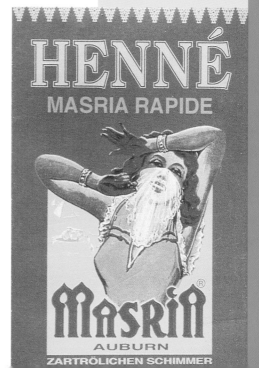

[milk and
almond pastilla]

Serves 6-8
Prep and cooking time:
1 hour

1¼ cups milk
4 egg yolks
1 egg
1 cup sugar, divided
3 tablespoons potato flour
   (e.g. potato starch)
1 tablespoon orange blos-
   som water
6 tablespoons butter
8 ounces skinned almonds
1 tablespoon ground
   cinnamon
Oil for frying
12 sheets phyllo
   pastry dough

In a saucepan, heat milk. Beat egg yolks and whole egg with ½ cup of the sugar. Add potato flour and pour boiling milk over this mixture, while stirring briskly. Then pour everything into the saucepan and bring to a boil, while stirring constantly. Boil for 3 minutes. Remove from heat and add orange blossom water. Then add 4 tablespoons of the butter cut into bits and stir until butter is fully mixed in. Let cool.

Brown almonds in the remaining butter then chop at high speed in a blender or food processor just long enough to chop them coarsely, but not to reduce them to a powder. Combine with the remaining sugar and cinnamon.

In a large frying pan, heat frying oil. Cut sheets of phyllo to be about the same size as the pan. Fry sheets of pastry two at a time for a few seconds so that they become golden, then drain on paper towels.

A few minutes before serving, preheat oven to 200°F. Place 2 sheets of phyllo pastry dough on an ovenproof dish. Spread with a little of the cream and sprinkle with almonds. Cover with another 2 sheets of phyllo pastry dough, spread with more cream, followed by more almonds. Continue until all ingredients have been used, topping with 2 sheets of phyllo pastry. Place in the oven and warm several minutes.

[fish briouats]

Serves 4
Prep and cooking time:
40 minutes

12 ounces white fish fillets
  (such as cod)
5 sprigs fresh parsley
2 cloves garlic
3 pinches mild chili powder
3 pinches ground cumin
1½ teaspoons lemon juice
1½ teaspoons oil
Salt
4 sheets phyllo pastry
  dough
1 egg white, beaten
Oil for frying

For serving:
3 tablespoons lemon juice
Chili powder

Place fish fillets in a saucepan with cold salted water, heat slowly just to the point of boiling, then cover, remove from heat and let cool.

Wash parsley sprigs, dry and chop leaves. Peel garlic cloves and squeeze through a garlic press.

Drain fish fillets, break apart flakes of meat and place in a bowl along with parsley, garlic, chili powder, cumin, lemon juice and oil. Season with salt and stir.

Fold each sheet of phyllo in half lengthwise, then in half widthwise. Place a quarter of the fish filling in the center of each sheet of pastry. Fold the bottom edge over the filling and then fold the two sides over the filling. Brush the top edge with egg white and fold this over too, making square "little letters."

In a large frying pan, heat frying oil. Fry the briouats for 3 minutes on each side, or until they are golden. Drain on paper towels. Serve hot with lemon juice seasoned to taste with chili powder.

[sausage briouats]

Serves 4
Prep and cooking time:
20 minutes

8 merguez or other hearty
  cooked sausages
8 sheets phyllo pastry
  dough
1 small egg white
Oil for frying
Harissa (see page 33)

Place 1 merguez one third of the way from the bottom of each sheet of pastry. Fold the bottom over the sausage, then fold the two sides in over the sausage. Roll the sheet toward the top, pulling it very tight and leaving the last quarter of the sheet exposed.

Gently beat the egg white with a fork to liquefy it. Brush onto exposed part of the sheet of pastry and finish rolling it up, pressing down to seal it tightly.

Heat frying oil. Fry briouats a few at a time and let brown several minutes. Drain on paper towels and serve immediately with harissa.

[shrimp briouats]

In a small saucepan, melt 1 tablespoon of the butter. Add flour and stir 30 seconds with a wooden spoon. Gradually add milk, stirring constantly. Bring to a boil while continuing to stir and simmer for 1 minute over low heat. Add salt, pepper and chili powder, overseasoning slightly so flavor comes through in finished product.

Add shrimp to sauce and stir. Let cool.

Fold phyllo dough in half lengthwise, then in half lengthwise again, to obtain 1-long-thin strip (about 5 inches across and 12 inches long). Lightly brush top strip with oil. Place a quarter of the shrimp filling at the bottom of each strip of pastry, in the center, and fold one corner of dough over the filling. Continue folding the bottom corner up, retaining a neat, triangular shape until you get to the top. Place a bit of oil on the top edge and fold under to make a neat package (see top illustration on page 89).

Heat oil and add the remaining butter. When butter becomes foamy, brown briouats about 4 minutes on each side. Remove, using a wide, perforated spatula and drain on paper towels. Serve piping hot.

Serves 4
Prep and cooking time:
30 minutes

2 tablespoons butter, divided
1 tablespoon flour
½ cup milk
Salt and pepper
Chili powder
6 ounces peeled shrimp
  (bay shrimp are fine)
4 sheets phyllo pastry dough
1 tablespoon oil

[crêpes with a thousand holes]

Makes 7–8 crêpes
Prep time: 5 minutes
Standing time: 2 hours
Cooking time:
2–3 minutes per crêpe

1½ cups flour
1 cup couscous
1 packet dried yeast
½ teaspoon salt
1 tablespoon oil

For serving:
Butter
Honey
Ground cinnamon

Combine all the ingredients except the oil, add about 1½ cups warm water and stir until a batter the same consistency as normal crêpe batter is formed. Cover and let stand for 2 hours in a warm place.

Heat a 10-inch nonstick frying pan and coat lightly with oil. Pour in 1 ladle of batter, tilting the pan to spread it around, and fry for 2–3 minutes over low heat. Small holes should form on the surface. Fry all the crêpes this way on one side, only, and let cool on a cloth without stacking them.

Smear crêpes with butter and honey, sprinkle with cinnamon and serve them right away!

[egg briouats]

Peel and chop onions. Wash parsley, dry and chop leaves.

In a frying pan, heat 1 tablespoon of the oil and braise onions. Sprinkle with sugar and a little salt and add cinnamon.

Break eggs into a bowl and beat with a fork. Mix with onions and remove from heat.

Fold phyllo in half lengthwise, then in half lengthwise again, to obtain 1-long-thin strip (about 5 inches across and 12 inches long). Lightly brush top strip with oil. Place a quarter of the egg filling at the bottom of each strip of pastry, in the center, and fold one corner of dough over the filling. Continue folding the bottom corner up, retaining a neat, triangular shape until you get to the top. Place a bit of oil on the top edge and fold under to make a neat package (see top illustration on page 89).

Heat the remaining oil and add butter. When butter becomes foamy, brown briouats for about 2–3 minutes on each side, a few at a time. Drain on paper towels. Serve piping hot with a small dish of sugar and cinnamon mixed together.

Makes 20 briouats
Prep and cooking time:
50 minutes

12 ounces onions
4 sprigs Italian parsley
4 tablespoons oil, divided
1 teaspoon sugar
Salt
1/3 teaspoon ground
  cinnamon
5 eggs
10 sheets phyllo
  pastry dough
Oil for brushing
2 tablespoons butter
Ground cinnamon
Salt

For serving:
2 tablespoons sugar
1 teaspoon ground cinna-
mon

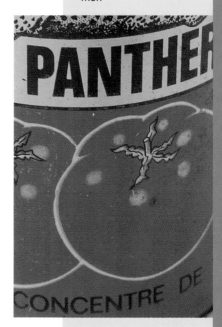

Briouats à la kefta, like any other briouats, are ideal for a buffet or picnic. All that matters is that they not be served too cold. Wrap them well to keep warm.

[briouats with spiced ground meat]

Peel and finely chop onion. Wash cilantro and parsley, dry in paper towels, and remove leaves and chop. Mix onion, cilantro and parsley with ground meat and add all the spices, and salt and pepper.

In a frying pan, heat 1 tablespoon of the oil. Sautè the meat mixture over low heat, stirring constantly with a spatula and pressing down on the meat until all the juice has been cooked out.

Break eggs into a bowl and beat with a fork. Remove meat from heat and mix in the eggs.

Fold phyllo in half lengthwise, then in half lengthwise again, to obtain 1-long-thin strip (about 5 inches across and 12 inches long). Lightly brush top strip with oil. Place a quarter of the shrimp filling at the bottom of each strip of pastry, in the center, and fold one corner of dough over the filling. Continue folding the bottom corner up, retaining a neat, triangular shape until you get to the top. Place a bit of oil on the top edge and fold under to make a neat package (see top illustration on page 89).

In a frying pan, heat the remaining oil. Add butter and when it becomes foamy, fry the briouats a few at a time until they are nicely golden (takes about 3 minutes per batch). Drain on paper towels. Serve hot with a small dish of sugar and cinnamon mixed together.

If you prefer, you can also cook briouats in a deep fryer.

Serves 4 or makes
20 briouats
Prep and cooking time:
45 minutes

1 small onion
2 sprigs fresh cilantro
2 sprigs fresh parsley
8 ounces ground beef
 or lamb
1 pinch ground cinnamon
1 pinch turmeric
1 pinch ground cumin
Salt and pepper
3–4 tablespoons
 oil, divided
2 eggs
10 sheets phyllo
 pastry dough
2 tablespoons butter

For serving:
2 tablespoons sugar
1 teaspoon ground
 cinnamon

[kefta pastilla]

Serves 6
Prep time: 40 minutes
Cooking time:
30 minutes

1 large bunch fresh parsley
1 onion
4 eggs
Salt and pepper
1¼ pounds boneless
leg of lamb
2 teaspoons ground
cinnamon
8 tablespoons butter
10 sheets phyllo pastry dough

Wash parsley, dry in paper towels and finely chop leaves. Peel and grate onion. Break eggs into a bowl, beat with a fork and generously add salt and pepper.

Cut meat into cubes and grind in a meat grinder with a medium cutter (or have your butcher grind it for you). In a large bowl, combine ground meat, parsley, onion, cinnamon, salt and pepper and knead it all together thoroughly. Add eggs and mix carefully.

Preheat oven to 400°F.

Melt butter and pour it into a cup, eliminating the white sediment. Butter a 10–12-inch baking pan (preferably a false-bottom pan) and assemble the pastilla (see pages 75 and 116) but without inserting intermediate layers of pastry. Make the surface as even as possible before positioning the last sheets, then brush melted butter over the top.

Bake in the oven for 40–50 minutes until the pastilla is crisp and golden. Serve immediately.

You can also make a pastilla every bit as delicious as this one using marbled beef, such as sirloin.

[folding briouats]

To make square briouats in the form of "little letters", proceed as follows: Fold each sheet of phyllo in half lengthwise, then in half widthwise. Place filling in the center of each sheet of pastry, gently flattening filling. Fold the bottom edge of the sheet that is closest to you over the filling, and then fold the two sides in, over the filling. Brush the top edge with egg white and fold this over too, tucking in or folding any excess dough to make a neat packet.

briouats **square (little letters)**

**cylindrical (cylinders)
briouats**

To make a cylinder, first fold each sheet of phyllo pastry in half and place lengthwise on the work surface. Place a line of filling on the bottom edge of each sheet. Fold the two ends of the pastry over the filling, then roll it up tightly. Brush the last bit of pastry with a beaten egg white or egg yolk mixed with a little water to seal the cylinder.

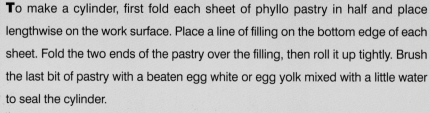

To make triangular briouats: Fold phyllo in half lengthwise, then in half lengthwise again, to obtain 1-long-thin strip (about 5 inches across and 12 inches long). Lightly brush top strip with oil. Place a quarter of the shrimp filling at the bottom of each strip of pastry, in the center, and fold one corner of dough over the filling. Continue folding the bottom corner up, retaining a neat, triangular shape until you get to the top. Tuck the last protruding bit of pastry inside (see top illustration on page 89).

Add cinnamon and, if desired, the orange blossom water to the almond paste and knead until well-combined.

Fold the sheets of phyllo pastry in half lengthwise, then in half lengthwise again, then prepare triangular briouats (see page 89). Pour honey into a large bowl.

Heat oil for frying. Fry briouats a few at a time, letting them brown for about 3 minutes. Drain, pat dry with paper towels and soak them immediately in the honey. Drain them again and arrange them on a serving dish. Serve cold on the same day or within the next 2 days.

Serves 4 or makes
20 briouats
Prep time: 40–50 minutes

12 ounces almond paste
  (homemade, see page 114;
  ½ recipe is needed)
½ teaspoon ground cinnamon
1 tablespoon orange blossom
  water (optional)
20 sheets phyllo pastry dough
1 cup honey
Oil for frying

[almond briouats]

After the ritual, washing of hands, a Moroccan meal generally

starts with a pastilla. This is followed by the méchoui

(spit roasted lamb or chicken), the tagines and finally the

couscous. Each guest should take a taste from every dish,

serving themselves from the main dish, using their thumb

and first three fingers of their right hand. Water is served

as the beverage. After washing their hands once more,

they finish the meal with a mint tea ceremony.

[quail and mushroom pastilla]

Serves 6:
Prep time: 1 hour
Cooking time: 1½ hours

2 onions
10 packaged quail
2 tablespoons butter
1 teaspoon turmeric
Salt and pepper
1 pound mushrooms
2 tablespoons lemon juice
3 sprigs fresh cilantro
2 sprigs fresh parsley
6 eggs
3 pinches freshly
   grated nutmeg

For assembling the pastilla:
3 tablespoons butter
10 sheets phyllo
   pastry dough

Peel and chop onions. In a casserole, combine onions with quail, butter and turmeric. Season with salt and a generous amount of pepper. Heat slowly while stirring. Add ¾ cup water, cover, and simmer for 50 minutes.

In the meantime, clean mushrooms and slice into cross sections. Sprinkle with lemon juice. Wash cilantro and parsley, dry in paper towels and chop the leaves.

When quails are tender, remove from the casserole. Add mushrooms, cilantro and parsley to the casserole. Simmer several minutes, then uncover the casserole and reduce the sauce until thick.

Break eggs into a bowl and beat with a fork. Season with salt and add nutmeg. Remove the casserole from heat, add eggs and stir. Heat casserole over very low heat and continue stirring until you have a smooth cream, then stop cooking.

Debone quail. Preheat oven to 400°F. Melt butter and pour it into a cup, eliminating the white sediment. Butter a 12-inch baking pan (preferably a false-bottom pan) and assemble the pastilla (see pages 75 and 116) but without inserting intermediate layers of pastry. Top with the last buttered sheets of pastry, tucking the edges down into the tin to form the "hem." Brush with melted butter. Bake for 30 minutes in the oven until the pastilla is a deep golden color.

Makes 20 briouats
Prep and cooking time:
30–40 minutes

1 bunch Italian parsley
10 ounces fresh
  goat cheese
1 tablespoon paprika
  or mild chili powder
Salt to taste
2 eggs
1 egg white
20 sheets phyllo
  pastry dough
Oil for frying

[goat cheese briouats]

Wash parsley, dry and chop leaves. Combine cheese, parsley and paprika or chili powder, and season with a little salt.

Break the two whole eggs into a bowl, beat with a fork and add to cheese mixture.

Gently beat the egg white with a fork to liquefy it.

Cut phyllo sheet in half widthwise, then fold this half in half lengthwise. Position lengthwise on a work surface, and place a line of filling on bottom edge and roll tightly into cylinders (see page 88). Brush the last part with a little egg white before rolling it all the way up to seal it.

Just before serving, heat oil for frying. Fry briouats a few at a time, letting them brown for about 3 minutes. Drain on paper towels and serve them immediately.

desserts

desserts

sweet and spicy

Almonds, honey, sugar, dried fruits and preserves are the main ingredients of Moroccan pastries, which are often served with mint tea. But Morocco's sweetness is also manifested in the ever present taste of orange blossoms and a wide variety of refreshing beverages based on almonds and fruit juices, as well as orange salads spiced with a touch of cinnamon.

Makes about 1 quart
Prep time: 15 minutes
Steeping time: 1 hour

1 pound skinned almonds
1 cup sugar, divided
1–2 tablespoons orange
  blossom water

[almond milk]

Process almonds in a blender or food processor with half the sugar, stopping before the almonds are reduced to oil. Pour the coarse powder formed into a bowl and crush it a little more to make it very fine.

Dissolve the remaining sugar in 1 quart of the water. Pour into bowl with almonds and let steep for 1 hour in a cool place.

Strain contents of bowl through a sieve lined with gauze, pressing it through with a pestle or wooden spoon. Add orange blossom water. Serve ice cold.

[gazelles' horns]

Makes 14 horns
Prep time: 45 minutes
Cooking time: 15 minutes

1 pound almond paste
   (homemade, see page
   114; ²/₃ recipe is needed)
3 tablespoons butter,
   divided
1²/₃ cup flour
Salt
3 tablespoons orange
   blossom water
1 egg white

Divide almond paste into 14 walnut-sized pieces and roll each piece into a thin sausage shape with tapering ends.

Prepare the dough: Melt 2 tablespoons of the butter. Place flour in a large bowl, forming a well in the center. In this well, pour melted butter along with 1 pinch salt and half the orange blossom water. Mix together while gradually adding the remaining orange blossom water until you have a firm and uniform dough (if dough is crumbly, slowly add up to ¼ cup of room temperature water, until dough becomes firm).

Divide this dough into 14 pieces so they are easier to roll out. On a lightly floured work surface, roll out each piece with a rolling pin into a thin circle, about 2½–3 inches in diameter.

Place almond paste sausages in a row along the top third of each circle of dough. Dampen the free area of the dough and fold it over the almond paste filling, pressing the edges together to seal. Use a pastry wheel to cut around the lumps of filling and to serrate the edges, then slightly curve each horn into a crescent shape.

Preheat oven to 350°F. Use the remaining butter to butter a baking sheet.

Place gazelles' horns on the baking sheet. Pierce each one several times with a knitting needle or the prongs of a fork, then brush with beaten egg white.

Bake for about 15 minutes in the oven until the gazelles' horns are just barely colored.

[almond cookies]

Chop almonds. In a large bowl, whisk egg and 2 cups of the powdered sugar until it becomes a uniform mixture.

Scrub lemon under warm water, dry and grate the rind. Add almonds, lemon rind, vanilla and baking powder to egg mixture and mix thoroughly.

Preheat oven to 350°F. Cover a baking sheet with baking parchment and butter the parchment. Dust a work surface with the remaining powdered sugar.

Grease your hands with a little oil. Take a walnut-sized piece of dough, roll it into a ball and then flatten it on the work surface. Place it on the baking parchment with the sugared side up. Repeat until all the dough is used, making sure to leave a space of 1–1½ inches between the dough pieces.

Bake for 15–20 minutes in the oven. Transfer ghoribas to a wire rack using a spatula and let cool.

You can also make shortbread ghoribas: Gradually mix 2⅔ cups flour with 8 ounces soft butter and ¼ cup powdered sugar. Roll dough into a ball and set aside for at least 2 hours in a cool place. Then put dough through a meat grinder and knead it. Taking walnut-sized pieces of dough, follow the same procedure as for almond ghoribas.

Makes 25 ghoribas
Prep time: 30 minutes
Cooking time:
15–20 minutes

12 ounces skinned almonds
1 egg
2⅓ cups powdered
  sugar, divided
1 lemon
½ teaspoon pure
  ground vanilla
½ teaspoon baking powder
Butter to grease
  parchment paper
Oil to grease hands

[fig flan]

Serves 4
Prep time: 15 minutes
Cooking time: 1 hour
Refrigeration time:
at least 2 hours

8 figs
2 teaspoons butter
Ground cinnamon
5 eggs
⅓ cup sugar
2 pinches ground vanilla
1½ cups milk

Preheat oven to 300°F. Wipe figs with a damp cloth, remove stem and break each fig in two. Butter a gratin dish and arrange figs on the bottom, round side down. Sprinkle with cinnamon.

In a large bowl, beat eggs, sugar and vanilla. Add milk and mix thoroughly. Cover figs with this mixture and bake for 1 hour in the oven in a bain-marie* until the cream has set.

Let the flan cool, then refrigerate for 2 hours. Serve very cold.

*Create a bain-marie (double boiler) by pouring boiling water into an ovenproof dish large enough to hold a gratin dish. Water should come about halfway up the side of the dish. Place dish with water in the preheated oven.

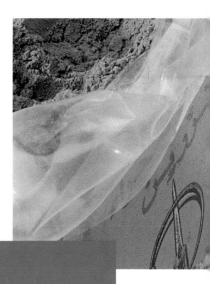

[couscous cookies]

Makes 25 cookies
Prep time: 30 minutes
Cooking time:
15–20 minutes

3 eggs
1¼ cups granulated sugar
1 cup warm melted butter
4 teaspoons butter, additional
1 teaspoon yeast
1 teaspoon vanilla
1 pound semolina,
    (about 3½ cups; add
    more if needed)
Orange blossom water
2 tablespoons
    powdered sugar

Whisk eggs and granulated sugar. Add melted butter, yeast and vanilla and mix. Pour in semolina and mix thoroughly, using a wooden spoon. Add a bit more semolina, if needed to make a stiff dough.

Preheat oven to 350°F. Use additional butter to butter one or two baking sheets. Moisten your hands with orange blossom water. Take a generous walnut-sized piece of dough, roll it into a ball and flatten it. Dip one side in powdered sugar and place on a buttered baking sheet with the sugared side up. Repeat until all the dough is used.

Bake for 15–20 minutes in the oven. Transfer cookies to a wire rack and let cool.

[orange blossom salad]

Peel 5 oranges, cutting all the way to the flesh. Cut into thin round slices and remove seeds. Squeeze juice from the remaining orange. Arrange orange slices on a serving dish. Sprinkle with orange blossom water and 3 tablespoons of the juice from the fresh orange. Dust first with powdered sugar, then with cinnamon. Refrigerate and let marinate for at least 1 hour.

In the meantime, brown slivered almonds in an ungreased, nonstick frying pan.

Just before serving, sprinkle almonds on top of the oranges. Garnish with several mint leaves if desired.

Serves 4
Prep and cooking time:
15 minutes
Marinating time: at least 1 hour

6 oranges
2 tablespoons orange
  blossom water
3 tablespoons powdered sugar
1 teaspoon ground cinnamon
2 tablespoons slivered almonds
Several fresh mint leaves
  (optional)

Serves 8
Prep time: 45 minutes
Cooking time: 40 minutes

8 tablespoons butter
1 pound skinned almonds
¾ cup sugar
1 tablespoon ground
   cinnamon
3 tablespoons orange
   blossom water, divided
Sheets phyllo pastry dough
   (about 1 pound)
1 pound honey

[baklava]

Melt butter and pour into another container to remove the sediment that forms.

Toast almonds in an ungreased, nonstick frying pan. Crush coarsely. Add sugar, cinnamon and 2 tablespoons of the orange blossom water.

Using a brush, butter a square or rectangular baking pan. Trim sheets of phyllo pastry to fit the pan.

Brush melted butter on 6 sheets of phyllo pastry on one side only and layer them in the tin. Cover with half the almond filling. Layer another 5 buttered sheets of pastry. Cover with the remaining filling and top with 8 buttered sheets of pastry. Sprinkle a little water over the top. Cut into diamond-shaped pieces.

Preheat oven to 400 °F.

Bake for about 30 minutes until the baklava is slightly golden. Heat honey and the remaining orange blossom water and pour over baklava while it is still hot.

[preserved orange rind]

Scrub oranges under warm water and dry. Cut rind into quarters from top to bottom, remove and cut into strips about ½ inch wide.

Place rinds in a pressure cooker, cover with a generous amount of cold water, close and cook for 8 minutes after the valve begins to hiss.

Remove rinds and plunge into cold water. Dry completely and weigh. In a preserving pan, combine orange rinds with their equal weight in sugar, cover with water and bring to a boil. Boil until all the water has evaporated, shaking the pan occasionally, but without using a spoon.

Pour the rinds into a dish and shake them to separate the strips from one another. Let cool. Place in a canning jar with coarse sugar (sugar crystals), close and shake the jar to coat the rinds with the sugar crystals. You can keep these preserves in a dry place for up to 1 month.

Prep time: 30 minutes
Cooking time: about 1 hour

Oranges with thick rinds
Sugar

[mint tea]

Rinse a teapot with boiling water. Wash mint leaves and dry carefully.

Place tea in a teapot, pour in 1 glass boiling water, then pour out water.

Crumple the mint leaves in your hands, put them in the teapot, fill it with actively boiling water (about 2 cups) and add sugar to taste. Cover teapot with a tea cozy and let steep for 5 minutes.

Stir briskly with a spoon, crushing the mint a little and testing the taste. Pour piping hot tea from a height into the glasses.

Serves 4–6
Prep and cooking time:
10 minutes
Steeping time: 5 minutes

1 handful fresh mint leaves
3 teaspoons green tea
Sugar cubes

These delicate pastries are delicious served with mint tea, which is poured from a height not in order to show off, but to make it frothy and enhance the flavor. Try it—it's all in the wrist!

[almond cigars]

Makes 24 cigars
Prep and cooking time:
1 hour

1 pound almond paste
  (homemade, see page
  114; ⅔ recipe is needed)
24 sheets phyllo
  pastry dough
1 egg white
Oil for frying
½ cup honey

Shape almond paste into 24 sticks about 6 inches long and slightly thicker than a cigarette. Place each stick one third of the way from the bottom of a sheet of pastry, fold over the bottom and then the two sides and roll it up. Brush the last part of pastry with lightly beaten egg white to seal it.

Heat frying oil to 350°F. In a small saucepan, warm honey. Drop cigars in hot oil a few at a time and let brown. Drain and dip them one by one in the warm honey using tongs. Arrange them in a pyramid.

You can also prepare almond cigars by wrapping them in the same dough used for gazelles' horns (see page 98) or in puff pastry rolled out very thinly, and bake in the oven at 350°F.

[stuffed dates and walnuts]

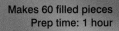

Makes 60 filled pieces
Prep time: 1 hour

30 dates
12 ounces almond paste
(homemade, see page 114;
½ recipe is needed)
Several drops green
food coloring
Several drops red
food coloring
60 walnut halves

Dry dates, cut open lengthwise and remove pits.

Divide almond paste into thirds. Add several drops green food coloring to one third and several drops of red food coloring to another third and knead the paste to obtain a uniform color.

Form each third of the paste into a long roll and cut each roll into 20 pieces. Stretch individual pieces out a little and insert one piece into each date in place of the pit. Sandwich one bit of almond paste between 2 walnut halves.

Place filled fruit and nuts in pleated paper baking cups and arrange on a fancy serving dish.

[fromage blanc cigars]

Pour fromage blanc into a fine sieve lined with gauze or cheesecloth and leave for 2 hours until it is well drained.

Break whole eggs into a bowl and beat gently with a fork. Add 1 pinch salt and fromage blanc. Mix carefully.

In a high-sided frying pan or deep fryer, heat frying oil to 350°C. Gently beat egg white with a fork to liquefy it.

Fold phyllo sheets in half lengthwise, and place lengthwise on work surface. Place a little of the cheese mixture one third of the way from the bottom of each sheet of pastry, fold the bottom over the cheese and then the two sides, and roll it up almost to the top. Brush the last part of the pastry with lightly beaten egg white to seal it and finish rolling.

Drop cigars in frying oil a few at a time and let brown for about 3 minutes. Drain on paper towels and serve hot.

Makes 12 cigars
Prep and cooking time:
20–30 minutes
Draining time: 2 hours

8 ounces fromage blanc
2 eggs
Salt
Oil for frying
1 egg white
12 sheets phyllo
   pastry dough

Wrap the choke in gauze or cheesecloth and knot it. Heat milk, pour into a bowl and place gauze bag in the milk. Leave it there for 5 minutes, then squeeze it between your fingers above the milk to extract all the liquid. Cover bowl and let stand for 1–1½ hours in a warm place.

Refrigerate curdled milk and let chill. Serve the milk very cold.

You can also add sugar to the milk and flavor it with orange blossom water before heating.

Makes 2 quarts
Prep time: 10 minutes
Standing time: 1½ hours

2 tablespoons raw choke
  (spiky part at center
  of artichoke)
2 quarts milk

[curdled milk]

When organizing a Moroccan meal at home, your first

priority should be comfort. Moroccan tables are surroun-

ded by plump hassocks, carpets and cushions to ensure

that everyone is at ease. The lighting should be subdued,

preferably candles scented with spices. As a beverage,

Moroccan wines are an excellent choice as well as plenty

of mineral water served throughout the meal.

[almond cookies]

Just barely melt about 5 tablespoons of the butter and let cool. In a bowl, combine flour and sugar and form a well in the center. Place the egg, ground almonds, vanilla and baking powder in this well and stir. Mix in the warm, melted butter and knead, while gradually adding enough water to form a uniform dough the same consistency as bread dough.

Briefly rinse raisins, dry, add to dough and mix. Divide the dough into two equal parts, and then form each half into a roll with a 1½ inch diameter.

Preheat oven to 400°F. Butter a baking sheet with the remaining butter.

Place rolls of dough on baking sheet spaced 1½–2 inches apart and bake for 15 minutes in the oven, removing them before they become golden, and let stand overnight.

The next day, cut rolls into slices about ½ inch thick. Place slices on an ungreased baking sheet and brown for 10 minutes in the oven. You can keep these cookies for up to 1 week in an airtight container.

Makes about 30 cookies
Prep time: 30 minutes
Cooking time: 25 minutes
Standing time: 12 hours

6 tablespoons butter, divided
1⅔ cup flour
½ cup sugar
1 egg
2½ ounces ground almonds (about ⅓ cup)
2 pinches ground vanilla
2 teaspoons baking powder
½ cup raisins

[almond paste]

Just barely melt butter.

Combine almonds and sugar and place in a blender or food processor. Process until combined (mixture will be crumbly).

Place this mixture on a work surface and knead while adding orange blossom water and melted butter until mixture becomes a paste. Refrigerate until you're ready to use it.

Makes 1½ pounds
Prep and cooking time:
10 minutes

3 tablespoons butter
1 pound skinned almonds
⅔ cup sugar
2–3 tablespoons orange blossom water

Serves 8
Prep time: 30 minutes
Cooking time 25 minutes

6 tablespoons butter
5 ounces dates
½ cup walnuts
2 eggs
½ cup sugar
⅔ cup flour
1 teaspoon baking powder
1 tablespoon orange
  blossom water
½ teaspoon ground
  cinnamon

[date nut cake]

Preheat oven to 350°F. Butter a 12-inch baking pan. Cover the bottom with baking parchment and butter the parchment.

Remove pits from dates and chop coarsely. Place walnuts in a blender or food processor and process until a coarse powder is formed.

Melt the remaining butter. Whisk eggs with sugar. Mix in the flour and baking powder, then add melted butter, chopped dates, ground walnuts, orange blossom water and cinnamon.

Pour batter into the cake pan and bake for 25 minutes. Let cool on a wire rack before removing from the tin.

You can cut this cake into diamond shapes and serve with curdled milk (see page 112).

[glossary]

Brick: Very thin sheets of pastry that are very difficult to prepare, known by different names in different North African countries. They are usually sold in packages of 10 or 20 and can be obtained in the efrigerated section of supermarkets, from venders of olives, or in the fruit and dried vegetable section at markets, and in Middle Eastern delicatessens. Be sure to check the expiration date. Bricks dry out very quickly so don't take them out of the package until you're ready to use them. If you reseal the package very carefully, you can keep them in the refrigerator for up to 3 days. In place of brick pastry, you can substitute sheets of phyllo pastry available in Greek delicatessens.

Chile pepper, fresh: You will mainly find green chile peppers and red chile peppers. The smaller they are, the hotter they are. Remove the seeds under cold running water or while wearing gloves because they contain a fiery-hot substance. Avoid rubbing your eyes.

Chili powder: Several varieties are available from spice vendors and in specialty markets. Ground chili pepper and cayenne are usually hotter than most chili powder's found at local supermarkets. Paprika is generally mild and you can easily use it in place of mild chili powder.

"Feuilles de brick": sheets which are similar to phyllo pastry dough, but round. These are difficult to find in the U. S., but phyllo pastry dough can be purchased fresh at some specialty stores, and frozen at most supermarkets. A few notes on working with and handling phyllo dough:

- While some photographs in this book show recipes being prepared with the round "feuilles de brick" all the recipes can be made successfully with the rectangular phyllo dough, following instructions in the preparation method for each recipe.
- Phyllo dough is thin and can tear easily—especially along the edges if they become dry, but don't be afraid of it as phyllo is forgiving and patches well with a bit of melted butter as "glue." Dry edges can be cut off, or misted lightly with water and gently separated.
- There are approximately 18–20 sheets of phyllo dough in a 1 pound package, each about 12x20 inches. Store any unused phyllo in an airtight plastic bag in the refrigerator (don't freeze a second time). It's better to have more than you need in case a few sheets tear.

- If you're using frozen phyllo, defrost it in the refrigerator for 1 or 2 days to allow the sheets to separate easily (defrosting at room temperature causes the sheets to tend to stick together).
- Have a dry work surface, keep dough you are not using covered with plastic wrap or a towel, and don't work under a sunny window or heat vent as phyllo easily becomes dry when exposed to direct heat. Work as quickly as possible, and use a sharp knife or scissors for cutting.
- Unsalted, clarified butter produces the best results. To clarify butter, melt over low heat, skim foam from top and slowly pour into another container leaving milky solids on the bottom of the pan.

Ginger, fresh: This is a light brown root with a twisted shape that you do not necessarily have to peel if it is very fresh. Buy it in small quantities from vendors of exotic products or in Asian markets and store in the vegetable bin of your refrigerator.

Ginger, ground: Drying ginger and reducing it to a fine powder changes its properties. For this reason you should never substitute ground ginger for fresh ginger.

Ras el hanout: The name literally means the "summit" or "head of the shop," in other words, the best there is. This mixture, which is essential for the preparation of couscous, once contained more than 30 different spices and aromatics, including dried rose buds. Today it is often less complicated. You may be able to find this spice blend in a specialty store or purchase it from a Moroccan or Middle Eastern restaurant. If not, see a simple version on page 37.

Skinned almonds: If you only have almonds with the skins on, place them in boiling water for 2 minutes, drain and pinch them between your thumb and index finger one by one. The skin will come off very easily.

glossary

[index]

Almond(s)
briouats 90
cigars 106
cookies 100, 114
milk 97
and milk pastilla 78
paste 114
stuffed with pigeons 37
Artichoke(s)
and orange salad 23
stuffed 15

Baklava 103
Beef (see also Meat)
kebab 53
Briouats
almond 90
egg 82
fish 79
folding 88–89
goat cheese 93
preparing 88–89
sausage 79
shrimp 80
with spiced ground meat 84
Brochettes
fish 59
kefta 57

Cake, date nut 115
Carrot salad 17
Cheese, goat briouats 93
Chicken (see also Poultry)
and lamb couscous with
vegetables 62
steamed 70
stuffed with couscous
and raisins 49
tagine with lemons and
olives 39
Cookies
almond 100, 114
couscous 101

Couscous
breakfast, with cinnamon 70
cookies 101
fish 66
fish stuffed with 60
lamb and chicken, with
vegetables 62
onion and raisin 58
preparing 60
and raisins with chicken,
stuffed 49
seven-vegetable 65
squab 56
stuffing for poultry 68
Crêpes with a thousand holes 81

Date(s)
nut cake 115
and walnuts, suffed 109

Egg briouats 82
Eggplant
salad 28
tagine and lamb 36

Fig flan 101
Fish
briouats 79
brochettes 59
couscous 66
marinade 38
stuffed with couscous 60
stuffed with spinach 54
tagine 45
Flan, fig 101
Fromage blanc cigars 110

Gazelles' horns 98
Grapes with quail 48

Harissa 33
Hummus 16

Kebabs
beef 53
lamb 40

Lamb
and chicken couscous with
vegetables 62
and eggplant tagine 36
kebabs 40
shoulder-of-, méchoui 71
tagine with onions 46
tagine with prunes 34
Lemon(s)
and bell pepper salad,
preserved 29
leg of, stuffed 57
and olives with chicken
tagine 39
preserved in brine 40
Lentil (harira), hearty 20

Meatball tagine with
tomatoes 42
Meat (see also Beef)
spiced ground with briouats 84
Milk
almond 97
and almond pastilla 78
curdled 112
Mint tea 104
Mushroom and quail pastilla 92

Nut, date cake 115

Olive(s)
and lemons with chicken
tagine 39
salad 11
Onion(s)
with lamb tagine 46
and raisin couscous 58